101 QUADS

chris mansell

Puncher & Wattmann

Thorny Devil Press

The Visual Poetics series features poems with a speakable visual-verbal structure on the page.

First published in 2021

Published by Puncher and Wattmann
PO Box 279, Waratah NSW 2298

in association with

Thorny Devil Press
PO Box 19, Mayfield NSW 2304

http://www.puncherandwattmann.com
puncherandwattmann@bigpond.com
thornydevilpress@gmail.com

NATIONAL LIBRARY OF AUSTRALIA

A catalogue record for this book is available from the National Library of Australia

ISBN 9781925780451

acknowledgements

Some of these poems were written during October 2016 as part
of the 365+1 project while a guest for that month.
Others have been published in *Maintenant*, *Cordite*, *Overland* and *StylusLit*.

The poems are typeset in Prestige Elite.

contents

36	brain music	[the effect of music]
37	brilliant out	[the young man will go to war]
38	damned the lone	[on not liking the done for one]
39	dancer trip	[the thrilling stage]
40	despise drawing	[apollinaire and sense]
41	difference defy	[cutting to the quick]
42	education is no	[the teams will kill anyone]
43	evil as the abs	[the myth of rationality]
44	harping on ange	[the angels are laughing]
45	hate purifies	[on hate]
46	having despised	[apollinaire redux]
47	heartspill	[young men of the western front]
48	highlands flung	[home on the highlands]
49	in the dark	[the trees that were there]
50	it is a plea	[it is polite]
51	lust in the sudden	[eros and thanatos]
52	midnight in	[midnight in the nursing home]
53	mine name	[those with my name]
54	no veto	[the failed dream of autonomy]
55	not every thing	[falling fruit]
56	overt champions	[hubris]
57	political party	[losing political will]
58	running numbers	[the daily chances]
59	smother up take	[after error]
60	stripped authentic	[the future comes]
61	stunned silence	[battle]
62	summer spilt	[summer comes]
63	the emptynedded	[that irish boy ned]
64	the scream next	[the scream broke]
65	the slim slip	[australian pasts]
66	theft impossible	[on gravity]
67	tricolor	[the words escape]
68	wait waits wait	[waiting]
69	when the big	[on the death of a tree]
70	wild wolves old	[on migration]
71	you will be	[on evolution]
72	your back art	[on not disturbing his sleep]
73	spider under	[the secret spider]
74	never apologise	[do not apologise]
75	safer and happi	[on time]
76	simply living	[speaking of poetry]
77	not to blame	[on thinking we are not to blame]

78 human origins [genealogy]
79 appalled at [evolving again]
80 the smirk edges [the body thinking]
81 the short blade [falling into lust]
82 that means i [hard of grasping]
83 anchor mist [holding on]
84 she feels [she is the wolf]
85 pretty sure [on futures]
86 the anxious [the harp]
87 fate is smirk [on fate]
88 loving mathemat [on numbering]
89 anchor sweet [on staying]
90 or fly not to [on leaving]
91 square squantum [on the square]
92 erk angle dis [on acuteness]
93 trembleheart is [wild thought]
94 a gale of wrens [a gale of wrens]
95 bracken furl [the bushfire comes]
96 stammer stilt [unable to say]
97 dark net [forgotten stories]
98 bushwren ticky [on being wren]
99 it betrays it [on mortality]
100 that one not [wanting to possess]
101 it that final [the present tense]

notes on the quads

essay

VISUAL POETICS and 101 QUADS

Visual Poetics is a collaboration between Puncher & Wattman and Thorny Devil Press, presenting poems which have an inherent visual-verbal structural aspect as visual *spoken* poetics on the page. Visual spoken poetics. That is a line of definition drawn in the wide sands of the field of interrelationships between text and image, internationally, across millennia.

The title Visual Poetics is taken from the catalogue *Visual Poetics: concrete poetry and its contexts* (1989)[1] by Nicholas Zurbrugg, which includes a panoply of kinds. Our use of the term is more restricted.

The work of interest in this series is concerned with the nature of poetry as a printed entity which is articulate in the voicing of poetic thought while being integrated into a visual form that cannot be undone without losing the visual-verbal poem. Unlike illustrated poetry (poetry which is placed alongside pictures) or ekphrastic poetry (a vivid description or amplification of a work of art) or concrete poetry (much of which is silent), visual poetics integrates the seen and heard in what Richard Kostelanetz has called 'imaged words and worded images'.[2]

All written, printed, projected or screened poems necessarily include the graphic elements of typography and layout, and these can be manipulated to create hybrid visual-verbal constructions ranging from the literal to the abstract. In an early anthology *Concrete Poetry: a world view* (1968)[3] the editor May Ellen Solt admits that: "There are now so many kinds of poetry being labeled 'concrete' that it is difficult to say what the word means." She then states that: "The essential is *reduced language*" (her italics), and that 'the concrete poet is concerned with making an object to be perceived rather than read", with "some insisting upon the necessity for poetry to remain within the communication area of semantics, others convinced that poetry is capable of transmitting new and other information – purely aesthetic information." This sliding scale of linguistic clarity also applies to sound poetry, where the phonic may override the phonetic.

It is now more than fifty years since that anthology was published, and debates about definitions and categories remain fertile.

This series does not engage with language-like scribbling or letter cut-ups which cannot be spoken as a meaningful poetic text no matter how brief. Thus, all so-called 'asemic' or wordless work, which celebrates a vacuum of meaning as an opportunity for the reader, is excluded on the grounds that writing-like shapes may refer to language but are not language; any more than a carefully carved marble 'book' shape is a book. Abstracted letterforms are better considered as a form of expressive graphic art which refers to but cannot replace coherent printed words.

Books like *The Last Vispo Anthology: visual poetry 1998–2008* (2010)[4] are filled with figurative lettered abstracts which are attractive as pictures but have either no or minimal words. In an essay on visual poetry (page 207) Karl Kempton states that: "The contemporary visual poem is generally composed with assembled and/or disassembled language material" and this necessarily includes a lot of collage as well as invented glyphs and text attacks (forcing the intelligible back into the inarticulate). The anthology is full of useful essays which debate aspects of a complex field of creative practice with little grip in public imagination.

An added ingredient of complexity in contemporary word-image studies has been the increasing use of text by visual artists – from Jack Pierson's rearranged scrap commercial letters (Desire/Despair as a crucifix) and Tracey Emin's neon homilies to failed romance ("Never Again!"), to Barbara Kruger's phrases on graphic collages ("Your body is my battleground") and Jenny Holzer's supposedly ironic clichés ("Murder has its sexual side") – just to name four prominent Americans in a world wide tide of artwork under assorted curatorial titles such as text art, word art, painted language, and so on. If anything, visual artists have out-maneuvered, out-innovated and out-scaled visual poets to take control of the 'intermedia'[5] space between writing and art, as extensively illustrated in publications such as *Art and Text* (2009) and *The Word is Art* (2018).[6] Whether the wordy artworks (wordworks?) shown can be considered to be 'poetry' is an open question. Art stole the poem without bothering to read it. It stole the idea of 'poem' as concentrated language and chopped pieces out which would fit onto a wall. And usually words by someone other than the artist. Often the words are only meant to give a presence of readingness, not to be carefully read. Not to be savoured. An exception in demanded attentiveness might be Vernon Ah Kee's painting *becauseitisbitter* which consists of the complete poem 'In the Desert' (1895) by Stephen Crane, in block letters.[7] A lot more could be said about the word as art.[8]

The long and layered international history of pattern poetry before the twentieth century is illustrated in Dick Higgin's *Pattern Poetry: guide to an unknown literature* (1987)[9] where the key criteria for a pattern poem is that "the text and visual form interact". Higgins notes that the term visual poetry is often subsumed for library cataloguing under *concrete poetry*, whereas "that term should really be reserved for works from the 1950s and 1960s which use the alphabet". He also notes that pattern poetry has been constantly derided since time out of mind. "Ben Johnson (1573–1637) dismissed pattern poetry as 'a pair of scissors and a comb in verse' ",[10] and even George Herbert's famous Easter Wings (published posthumously in 1633) was belittled by Thomas Hobbes (1588–1672).[11] Higgins notes that: "... with little or no attention being given to the theoretical intricacies and potentials of pattern poetry as a visual or conceptual hybrid ... English pattern poetry, unsurprisingly, wanes in the late seventeenth century, and there is none known at all from the eighteenth."[12]

In the sixteenth century, many geometric shapes were considered suitable for pattern poetry including the rhombus, the triangle, the rondel or sphere, the egg and the square. With the cessation of such poetry in English for hundreds of years, the next example of a pattern poem usually pointed to is the 'Mouse's Tale' by Lewis Carroll in his novel *Alice's Adventures in Wonderland* (1865), a mimetic shape representing a mouse's tail. Guillaume Apollinaire's *Calligrammes* (1918) are similarly mimetic, using shapes such as a bird, a fountain, a horse, and that famous 'rain'. After George Herbert's, the next well-known non-representational geometric shape poems – after a gap of over three centuries – are Dylan Thomas's 'Vision and Prayer' (1944).[13] The first poem in a rhombus form starts with hearing a child being born in the next room: "Who / Are you / Who is born / In the next room / So loud to my own / That I can hear the womb / Opening and the dark run / Over the ghost and the dropped son / Behind the wall thin as a wren's bone? ..." The geometric form is achieved by variable spacing, with slight gaps within lines allowing the edges to symmetrically conform. 'Vision and Prayer' is not one of Thomas's great poems, though Allen Ginsberg writes in its praise on the Allen Ginsberg Project website in a section on pattern poems.[14]

John Hollander made a specialty of pattern poems in his book *Types of Shape* (1969),[15] including the shape of a swan and its reflection, a door key, a sideways heart and a sitting cat. Using a fixed width Courier font, differing line lengths create the outline. There are several geometric typographs, such as one in the shape of a six-pointed star.

Chris Mansell's *101 Quads* sit within solid traditions but she has made something new, using a strict geometric form of four inter-linked squares each made up of letters in a grid structure of fifteen letters across and eight lines down. Each one of the four stanzas in a quad is a formal typographic and geometric entity within which phrases fight for position in a descending spill-over. As geometric pattern poems, the quads thrive in an intermedia space where formal constraint plays enticing and enriching games with meaning and poetic speech, with each of the one hundred and one bringing out a distinct voice.

The quads are a must-read innovation in poetic form. The set of quadrilaterals' formal demands act as a device as restrictive as any traditional stanza form, from the sonnet and limerick to the villanelle.
Becoming spoken voice is at the heart of these poems. There are added audio elements as internal sound tracks made from letters in red type run simultaneously through lithe lines which remain bonded and bound to the grid. This double patterning is a score for another reading or sounding of each poem, bringing a resonate echo which varies in its level of abstraction from poem to poem.

Each poem demands its own way of being read and sounded, making for a lot to chew on and listen to. Complex speech patterns are established within a repeated geometric structure. Narrative threads spill over line breaks which disrupt their flow and enrich the experience with telling sounds, finding words inside each other, kicking and pecking like birds breaking out of a shell.

The quads aren't always 'easy', because of the unusual pattern of lines with words sometimes hanging over into the next line, but why should poetry be as instantly digestible as cornflakes? Once the reader adapts, the flow of (often double) meanings is steady and the rhythms become engaging. Some poems have a clear thread of 'story' to follow along, while others challenge what both poem and poet are doing with and through language itself. The quads are genuinely entertaining, and repay multiple readings.

Chris Mansell has stretched the boundaries of inherited forms to make distinctively fresh work. She has released limited edition artist books of the quads as they have developed over the past six years. A review by John Jenkins of the first of these, *Stung* (2014)[16], appeared in *Cordite*[17]. It is a great pleasure to introduce this important book *101 Quads* in its complete form, and to open its pages to both the eye and the ear of a wide readership.

Richard Kelly Tipping

References

[1] *Visual Poetics: concrete poetry and its contexts*, Nicholas Zurbrugg, Museum of Contemporary Art, Brisbane, 1989. Nicholas Zurbrugg (1947 – 2001) "an energetic advocate of postmodern expression" to quote from his obituary in The Guardian, untiringly investigated and promoted key issues and practitioners in the field of verbal-visual interchange. He is greatly missed by friends and colleagues. See for example his obituary at www.realtime.org/obituary-nicholas-zurbrugg

[2] *Imaged Words & Worded Images*, edited by Richard Kostelanetz, Outerbridge & Dienstfrey, USA, 1970. "Poetic imagery, artful poetry, concrete poetry and beat wordsmithing by Claes Oldenburg, Raul Hausmann, John Cage, Alan Kaprow, Merce Cunningham and others". This is a far wider field of interest than this Visual Poetics series can accommodate, but the phrase 'imaged words and worded images' is useful.

[3] *Concrete Poetry: a world view*, edited by May Ellen Solt, Indiana University Press, 1968.

[4] *The Last Vispo Anthology: visual poetry 1998–2008*, edited by Craig Hill and Nico Vassilakis, Fantagraphics Books, Seattle, 2010. Australian poets Tim Gaze, Gareth Jenkins, Pete Spence, Cornelis Vleeskens and Mark Young are included, representing a particular school of thought and practice in a diverse and active field in Australia which is populated by many other kinds of visual concrete poetry (by whatever names).

[5] Intermedia is a term used by Dick Higgins to discuss new relations between arts, as in poetry and painting interacting to become visual poetry, or painting and theatre interacting to become performance art.

[6] *Art and Text*, edited by Aimee Selby, Black Dog Publishing, London, 2009. *The Word is Art* by Michael Petry, Thames & Hudson, London, 2018.

[7] *becauseitisbitter*, Vernon Ah Kee, 2009. Painting, synthetic polymer on linen. Dimensions 240 x 320 cm. Collection of the Art Gallery of New South Wales, Sydney. The Gallery's website credits the poet, and notes that: "The work incisively articulates the role of art as a forum for radical agency."

[8] See for example my editorial in the special *The Word as Art* issue of *Artlink* (2007). The magazine includes discussion of many important word art practitioners in Australia.
Artlink, The Word as Art, edited by Richard Tipping, Issue 27:1, March 2007.
www.artlink.com.au/articles/2910/editorial/

[9] *Pattern Poetry: guide to an unknown literature*, Dick Higgins, SUNY, New York, 1987.

[10] *Ibid*, page 14, sourced as "Walsh 1925, page 271". In the bibliography this is given as: "Walsh, William Shepard. *Handy-book of literary curiousities*, 1895; Philadelphia; J.B. Lipincott, ca. 1925".

[11] *Ibid* page 14 "The royalist essayist Thomas Hobbes (1588–1672) attacks pattern verse as such but especially George Herbert in A discourse upon Gondibert … (1650, page 126)."

[12] *Ibid* page 14

[13] 'Vision and Prayer', Dylan Thomas (1944), verse one. Sourced from various websites, some

of which incorrectly reset the poem. Copyright expires in 2023, on the seventieth anniversary of his death. It is not pushing things too far to reproduce for study purposes the first of the poems, taken as a screengrab from a scan of the book published on visoundtextpoem.blogspot.com. Accessed 1 January 2020.

VISION AND PRAYER

I

Who
Are you
Who is born
In the next room
So loud to my own
That I can hear the womb
Opening and the dark run
Over the ghost and the dropped son
Behind the wall thin as a wren's bone?
In the birth bloody room unknown
To the burn and turn of time
And the heart print of man
Bows no baptism
But dark alone
Blessing on
The wild
Child.

[14] The Allen Ginsberg Project www.allenginsberg.org/2017/09/w-s-20/ Accessed 1 January 2020.

[15] *Types of Shape*, John Hollander, 1969. New edition by Yale University Press, 1991. For discussion see, for example: 'A Journey to Poetry of Geometrical Shapes from the Ancient Time to Poetry of John Hollander' by Mehrdad Moazami Goudarzi, Leila Baradaran Jamili and Bahman Zarrinjooee in the ***Journal of Novel Applied Sciences***, 2014, available at www.jnasci.org. Accessed 1 January 2020.

[16] *Stung*, Chris Mansell, Wellsprung Productions, 2014. This was the first book publication of any of the quads, containing about thirty.

[17] Stung by Chris Mansell – Review http://cordite.org.au/reviews/jenkins-mansell/

quads

somewhere not h
ere elsewhere n
ot us that othe
r those notus t
hat distinguish
ed those exting
uished to be th
ose other you k
now over away i
n our dark away
over the horizo
n over where th
e sun shines di
fferently darkd
ays for them da
rk dreams for u
s those heartac
hers with their
spears those st
range gods whic
h kill us thoug
h they do not e
xist those ordi
nary fools like
us believing th
e news our cere
monies of exalt
ed elseother no
not no there ar
e no here there
else where ther
e are no others

too much theref
ore too much th
erefore nothing
not much not so
me too much add
s makes nothing
not some not fr
agment too much

kills all overl
y entirely much
a little is alw
ays just a litt
er of much once
once another li
ttle until toge
ther much too m

any much breaki
ng in a waves t
oo many over ou
t of breath and
under breathing
much and little
cahoot collatin
g many to muchm

ass before brea
th is can befor
e breathing pos
sible before li
minal little me
rge and mass bl
ots more than b
ecome is a much

as present as l
ightning splint
opened wound cr
acked the blood
and fire impati
ence havingtobe
there volte fac
e earthingstrik

e this is how i
t really the sm
ackbang brightb
looded donotget
inmyway lightfi
re easy to beli
eve in gods and
fury but this i

s worse a harde
r lesson a unpe
rsoned cosmos n
othing to do wi
th us harm or g
ood overrid cas
ual as sex ruth
less flowing in

evitable standi
ng alone in a f
ield in the sto
rm you might be
fucked you migh
t be pierced by
the indifferent
universe or not

time folded bac
k at abduls leb
anese restauran
t or takeaway c
orner elizabeth
and cleveland t
hree hippies we
used to be with

flares and hair
and rings and b
adges always tw
o aspirant male
s and one tight
panted adorable
all her she the
desired is safe

ty for the boys
the want but he
sitate the othe
r bloke the exc
use and she wan
ting this one o
nly the fizzspa
rk of desire ma

kes the monarch
s of all the wo
rld that was us
even the clothe
s are ours then
we stole thenno
w silversings f
lares abduls is

one in one with
in only sole th
e two the secre
ted one insider
hider not danci
ng quiet watchf
ul as a snake c
oiled watcha go

tcha look out c
oiled up as a s
pring for impin
ge and recoil t
hat one clamped
inside the dayl
ight night over
cover one so sm

ooth to the tou
ch so hungry fe
eding on the su
nmoon and baski
ng in the ask a
m i the beautif
ul one of all h
eartplease insi

de the crimp an
d noli me tange
re of fragile e
ternal that unt
ouched thing kn
own and fled th
e pulsing crime
life insided in

the burden of f
reedom is to ha
ve and having t
oo much its hor
izons too far a
nd beaches whit
er more white t
han thought all
ows the sun spa
rring with glor
ygreen benign f
reedom claws in
sidious onto ou
r craving backs
oh freedom agai
nst what do i s
truggle excepti
ng guilt of ple
nty louche unkn
owing disconnec
t we know to be
akmatova is not
us never so bra
ve to take igno
my of silence n
ot brave enough
to stand up but
forever crouchi
ng afraid on th
e shore nice in
the sun too fea
rful to be poet

it is notmemory
not prefrontall
y formal not wo
rdy talky not n
o the soft hipp
ocampus the amy
gdala the warmt
h or the fearbo
und dog brain b
irdinstinct wat
er fog upseepin
g wordless know
untrusted kindl
ing not to be a
rguedwith but w
ise to dangerfe
ar before memor
y talks in grow
nup sentences s
ense to be talk
ed throughovers
always onandove
r meanwhile the
otherone person
mind knows or m
akes it up unti
dy memory tidie
d up and self a
drift between f
iction and argu
ment amemory un
thing unselfing

if you wanted y
ou could hear t
he empty in her
irishvoice keen
stringing throu
gh greener airs
and seasons lef
t and be the lo

nging seas of o
ver there never
seen again my d
aring darling d
aughterson rivi
ng the motherhe
art her keening
song a keen see

shall i not a s
ong so thin a s
lip of a thread
no more than th
inking wide and
the hard lipped
daughterson gon
e like a god in

to the dry coun
try of no one k
nown into the f
lat heatsmacked
plains with hor
izons so long t
hey burn your e
yes she singing

when the war en
ds the knot cut
the day unravel
led we will not
be human the ba
rbarians at the
gate will ditch
tents there chi

ldren will be b
orn ragged uned
ucated bereft o
f fear no one w
ill let them in
they will ask a
nd will be deni
ed and peace wi

ll settle as qu
iet as snow and
chill us to our
bones soon hill
s are borders a
nd streams path
s and the war w
ill stop and we

will not scheme
strive rive and
cheat darling s
words will fall
bombs rot in si
los calmpeace s
ettle and we wi
ll not be human

what you lookin
g at mate watch
choo watch choo
lookin lookin a
t you bloomface
blastbummed hoo
ligoonical bomb
astier shoutfac

ed bus stirring
noiseclapper be
llbadweather pi
mplearsed doped
odgy middlearse
primple watch c
hoo mate lookin
g you looking n

ot you other fo
ol twitchbummed
slope shouldere
d puttycoloured
blackyellow fro
gwop watch choo
bong bucket bim
boy angry manst

ick womanbag st
inkplug watch c
hoo who looking
you looking you
fatflatchestfoo
ted rateyed mag
gotwormer watch
you looking you

it is tangletri
p the privateer
language that u
ttering jangleu
r that jelly ho
ps through thos
e nounverbs and
spins a modifie

r not moderatel
y but songstopp
ed and poetlike
d the this is t
he other metaph
or shift that g
rammar slap bre
ak and stammeri

ng and shush to
speakeasying sh
ush to the craz
y talk the poet
ers run downhil
l and chase the
inevitable word
s mad they will

not be calm hoo
ning letting ou
t their fractur
etalk no making
them talk strai
ght down the ba
rrel for poem t
he word go back

unsinge the opa
l tear out that
broken fire str
ip that tenderl
ing from the br
east stopkisses
and savage alle
very flowerthin
gs draw the lin
e straight fixe
d and correctio
n red unharness
grace skimp vis
tas and nevermi
nd that fucking
rainbow too man
y of them and s
uch a light wei
ght apology yes
forget that and
softlies forget
those too shape
s of things rid
iculous quietly
what purpose se
rves that forge
t it all sum up
rule over stand
behind with kni
ves and in fron
t with saluting
smarmly do that

is brilliant is
is shining scin
tillating light
blasting good s
o much good alm
ost bad and fat
e being what sh
e is her motive

s all ways susp
ended belief in
she will be rig
ht because fate
you know her wi
ll knock your s
ockets out good
will turnout ba

d and a bad day
will change lif
e to good and y
ou there standi
ng gogglemouths
lacking and fat
e she is shinin
g and not an in

ch perturbed wo
rlds or words a
re allthesame t
o her meanwhile
that trick of h
ers has gobwopp
ed you knowever
she laughing is

he so keen ache
s like a boy th
e backyard blow
out bowling bli
tzing he the he
ro and dazzle l
ike tv like mov
ies notcaring c
harm beautifull
y rich competen
t o happy skies
this the plan n
ot lone hesitat
e not cripplegu
tshy now finall
y normal a norm
al man in norma
l clothes stand
ing in a normal
park with dog b
all sunshine ph
otogenic hair n
ow his arm rais
ed with ball th
e dog sprungtig
ht watching the
normal man thro
ws and the spru
ngtight dog wat
ches daylight d
ogstill man fet
ches it himself

the otherness o
f things a surf
ace so impermea
ble to the thou
ghts of mammals
and all those o
ther numinous s
olids we ambiti
ously adorecare
ss arrange dust
to feel the pul
sequick that we
hope is there i
n the pose of a
n anglepoise sh
iftyas an homun
culus coolas me
tal a little co
ckedhip thing o
r objects in di
smaldank taupes
each unrequired
unrequited thin
g sobeautifully
cruel enough to
make you cry we
want them to ad
ore our birthdy
ing selves they
resent needywan
ts dread our em
pathetic hearts

in the imaginar
y country there
were kings such
brave and begil
t such rich suc
h bloody murder
ous such incest
such strutwallo
w con con conni
vers ermined ma
fia triad bikie
thugs working w
ith pr geniuses
swordgore and m
ange a subsidia
ry of pillagera
pethieve conglo
merate internat
ional these hea
dlopping puffwe
asels need gods
to save them my
th to protect t
heir mortal dea
d forgot now th
e distant stumb
lythings remain
ing will we cry
when liz goes a
nd her gormless
sprog will goof
upon the stages

it is a bird mo
vement thing if
still then read
y to fly if fly
ing ready to fa
ll if falling r
eady to land if
waiting readyto
eat the life ou
t of blossom or
bug the immanen
t thing embodie
d promise its e
ye on you slomo
your earthlongi
ng feet and tim
estrung fears o
f death and sol
onesome awkward
ness what do yo
u become what r
eadiness are yo
u unbirded thin
g when unrestin
g are you mindf
lying and unafr
aid are you des
pairing for wan
t of wings imag
ine yourself an
angel you are n
ot us not us no

a chucklebird a
greengirl bounc
ing heavy bodie
d bowergirl she
knows she wants
his skinny shin
y arse that ave
nue parvenu but

baby blue until
another and she
too booty two s
he wants him to
he desperate an
d pretty quiver
nerved eagertop
lease as a brid

e he sings chru
cccckk and sexy
struts his neck
out do you do y
ou want to to t
o o they do the
y do those shin
y flanks that w

hoohoo blue she
the first comes
down to and too
she two comes t
oo but oo he is
the thing and s
oon more greeny
girls comeswoon

today we must b
elieve in sky t
he flighty fict
ion though dupe
d every day and
every night tha
t duplicity mak
ing naked the t

hin blue lie th
e cape of nothi
ng that comfort
ing blue we thi
nk is sky seems
safe and warm a
nd blue because
it is not sky i

t hides the dee
per darker othe
rness the far f
ired stars brea
thless galaxies
how small we fe
el how insifica
nt we say and c

lose our eyes t
he night sky so
hard distant we
are afraid want
our blanky back
our not sky clo
ud scry the day
closed and warm

the asphalt col
oured thing was
bones and pimpl
y featherbuds i
ts head allbeak
and eyes too sm
all tobe afraid
too edible to s
quark too far a
way from homene
st to live then
he and i reache
d for the highe
r toomuch and g
lebebooks ladde
r tooshort we s
cooped little g
rey to icecream
bucket drove th
ree suburbs got
another ladderl
ongenough and l
ittle greypimpl
eskin bulge eye
s scratchfooted
the bucket tryi
ng only now esc
ape but my hand
and his hand an
d he on the lad
der softly into
squarkface nest

do not have the
idea beforehand
do not strain i
t through the p
re of all prefr
ontal cortex do
not thinkonit w
orkit out ratio

cinate definite
ly do no ponder
s do no drownin
g in thought do
no hardest thin
ks concentrated
soft best ideas
climbing on you

like randy monk
eys pulling you
r hair stealing
your mindandcof
fee then ratars
ing away justas
you thought you
might you might

catch them in t
he act they shi
ton you great h
eight etc and e
venif you did g
et the monkey i
t has eaten all
the poems again

overwrought iro
n to the skin n
ip and tussle p
incer to the gr
ist scissors to
the throttler i
t is skin v met
al our worse in

vention iron sh
attering bronze
the limp curl o
f gold our most
beloved enemy p
in to skin need
le spline and h
arrow rack we a

dore it a truth
ful cleanse cut
and bladesunder
cleave and fork
pitch ready our
dangerous trans
u friend nickel
pale hidden and

explosive if an
noyed the subtl
eunsubtle pluto
nium neighbouri
ng palamericium
itching to do i
ts trembling fi
ssile metalbest

stick to stones
do break some p
oems but a verb
will always hur
l you wilding f
lowers will nou
n you down thos
adjectives dese
rt you metaphor
s will eat your
soul and simile
s do likewise b
ut doggerel wil
l bite your bum
and drain the b
rain politely g
erunds savage g
erunds they ing
you while you a
re sleeping a p
alindrome gives
no rest with it
s back and plod
dy forthing hec
kticklish synta
x runs amok and
hyphenation bor
es you colons f
art stops depar
t but misattrib
utions are real
awkward buggers

damn stumble th
e triphead sing
ledouble though
t intwo minds t
his or the othe
r trapped as li
zard battles ap
e and we are st

randed on the s
toop of think m
umblebrainly du
lly notchoosing
this or this or
worse a multitu
de of otherones
each menu harms

steak is more b
etter but beast
ly pasta more b
utter fat piggi
es are definite
ly but what i w
ant escapes the
thingfangle min

d does not mind
its desires doe
not know its na
me cannot clear
see itself want
s to other some
kind is stuck t
wixty as a blot

flatout moodlin
g songed out sk
inned and lanky
brained too laz
y to think up f
un too unned to
up too over out
to bother bliss
ing angst is en
nui if you care
d enough if the
slate is cleane
r or grubbier y
ou do not notic
e you do not wi
sh for anything
want nothing be
cause effort bo
res you no sold
iering on you a
re the deserter
too feckless to
front sunday is
all week forese
en so known and
safe this luxur
y of boredom th
is oasis of tri
te this glut of
please oceanful
cleanblooded du
llish frisunday

the shame at bl
ink stopstilled
overought shall
ishilly unthoug
ht the hero sel
f funked out no
bbled flatirone
d and spiritdry

that paralyse b
odyshame shockm
onster throttle
lock the body c
raw sticking br
eath cancelling
absence you are
not there selfi

sm an abstracti
on the animal a
bates limbs fin
d themselves br
ain unlocks the
mind heartspeed
the deadfaint o
f couldhavebeen

suddenly threed
imensional brig
and worldthieve
r gone loosed o
n the world els
ewhere the rovi
ng terror flatg
oes fear abroad

it is a hit a d
ip a ramoozling
top tip it is f
abbotastic this
grandee pleasan
t this unexpect
ed antiglum exu
berant outofthe
blue undeserved
extrabountifull
y somuch cannot
express this go
od luck not one
can know only b
ecause the boas
t because the t
oo much because
it seems fatete
mpting immodest
ly blessed this
secret joy sidl
ing in and slip
dunking delight
before you know
before kismetfa
te before extra
life a dimensio
n more and colo
ured bright thi
s thing this gi
ft so superstit
iously so right

a thrill a minu
et the dance du
jour your thril
ling body muscl
emusic straight
to the solo mio
jitterjams of l
ions and loinin
gs those drumme
rs making sex o
n their skins s
ax become saxie
r notes bluer a
ir so scarce we
breathe heavier
overtrill an tr
ill and flexhip
soon your mouth
and mine soon t
he summer hotsp
eed slick and s
ticky but the d
ance a piano ji
gs us up beatsk
ip pulse the so
ng marrows into
the bone hardda
ncing to soft m
use it new bars
open new songwa
ys atempo air a
nd lovers rests

outstumped that
tree once lorik
eetladen fullas
beauty striving
at the brim fal
ling in love wi
th a tree is ea
sy a person har
der they answer
back do not pur
ify the air thi
s tree was a th
ing entire ruth
lessly earthgri
pped its blosso
ms red and juic
y when they cle
ared the paddoc
k for the new r
oad they left i
t for awhile as
if they could n
ot bear then we
walked around i
t anciently our
witchcraft coul
ddo nothing mou
rning not enoug
h the prayers o
f rainbows also
not enough stum
ped and stilled

he is worriedab
out posterity t
hough posterity
the poster girl
of laughs is kn
itting warmth a
nd thinking not
atall of him sh
e is picking ra
bbits outof her
blackcopious ha
ir disposing ki
ngdoms makingun
making fabulous
filing the grin
s off sharks wi
thout success s
mug bastards me
anwhile poets s
tay up late wan
ting it to be t
hem please plea
se be ennobelle
d alas posterit
y looks the oth
er way does not
see she is long
sighted afteral
l but some nigh
ts she cannot s
leep for all th
e poets weeping

goodbye farewel
l adieu ooroo t
o you fast forw
ard gone the la
st gone tata by
eee so long and
those fish tood
looo for good g
one finish wrap
ped up over and
out last drinks
last stand make
tracks down the
road blow throu
gh bugger off i
n the offing pi
ss off shoot th
rough the midni
ght flit depart
my sweet melanc
holy ascent pac
k it up or in g
o to god left t
he building gon
e home shutup s
hutdown regretf
ully depart and
thanks for havi
ng me how evers
o you did duste
d done I am off
now with thinks

afternoon ferry
hips a wharf go
es feral in the
light a wondero
us jam of metal
and wood old as
churns chokes a
nd stops breath
ing diesel damn
ed dreams spilt
portside sharks
blister hopeful
as angels sharp
eyed for fallen
fruit oh artful
death you are a
sudden dancer s
o accurate blit
he and wily you
hide in the sun
shine scoop the
skim of days be
fore the armist
ice of age it i
s the quiet ter
ritory of shame
in being mortal
which drives us
to desire the s
hark nudges the
ferry hope jags
exits starboard

an ecstasy of o
ranges picked f
rom the tree fu
lfilled in thef
t the flesh eat
er stealing qui
vering fruit it
longs to be tak
en to be plucke
d devoured whol
e spat forth ma
ny seeds fallen
on the stony gr
ound the others
wait pick me pi
ck me their des
ire as silent o
range their rou
ndness rests su
llenly beautyfu
lly against the
sunlight that s
uckled them pic
k me pick me ea
t my juices suc
k me again tast
e my flesh give
me the sweet sa
voured agony of
my wishes eat o
h my saviour dr
ink eat save me

awake the sudde
n landfill of d
esire the rubbi
sh heart the he
and she she she
he he absurd he
at pulsing some
improbable thur

sday thirsty af
ternoon some no
thing comment o
r eye flight ar
moured heart up
and at it the s
ingle lagging a
t the gate list

en the scratchi
ng at the doors
the clamour and
clash at the ga
me warden heart
ready with blun
derbuss to shoo
t the old fashi

oned thing stil
l the avalanche
comes no gun or
shoulder to sto
p it coming aga
inst every will
the ground shif
ts falls you to

blurt harbinger
dawnday strappe
d sprung overed
ged red surpris
e whole planets
hift great heav
e brilliant aur
ora dangerfires

over every ordi
nary dawn darin
g overwhelms sk
y glisterrock s
hift and drag t
o far to imagin
e too far to th
ink of ordinary

extraordinary j
ust like a sham
e incredulous d
aylight over th
e brink unmerci
ful light danci
ng shift rockin
g space the tou

gh edge grandly
same perfect as
ever predictabl
e as art dawnth
rills standardl
y eastfire spin
dle of lightspe
ar overcomes no

brain music the
hollowed out cr
anium of notkno
wn the jingle b
ang thud and dr
umbells of conn
ect this only o
ur your our you
r brain its wor
dshifted exactl
y self ours unf
aithful to your
my controllers
wordfected gram
per gram edge a
nd cut directly
defibs tell lik
e it is the unt
rustable indest
ructible tellin
g counting outs
and ins of ever
and more but th
at beat straigh
t to the brains
tem straight to
our misundersta
king slender be
at animal we yo
u me will not a
dmit to if musi
c be muse dance

brilliant outpo
st building slo
ppy on sandy so
il the only way
to live is to s
teal broad brav
e as you can be
changing the de
stiny of erotic
war brutal free
dom creating ne
w countries nat
ions ideas buil
t over abundant
dictatorial cor
pses the glorio
us holding us i
n their cold ha
nds demanding g
lory let histor
y unhand us let
glory die gorml
ess gory gravel
y impotent last
posting fragile
bugle dust in t
he ears mercy o
n us mercy on t
hem may they st
ay safely depar
ted o darling s
oft skinned boy

damned the lone
ly piteous crin
ge hard stone o
f other over th
ere another pla
ce listen to th
e stones we hav
e become immora

l as bats scour
ing the sky for
echoes hungerin
g for stolen fr
uit to care not
enough the frag
ile words not e
nough knowing w

ithout dreaming
not enough doin
g never done en
ough and not ov
er we hate them
those lonely ov
er there the he
art broken bone

broken the styl
us fights the g
roove we hate t
hem those lonel
y they call out
pain in our ear
s we hate the l
one painful one

dancer trip sma
tter cut lights
shutter clapper
blink and light
slander the fra
ctured stage th
e brilliant lie
instant shafted

splice and leop
ard move slende
r ambisplit cut
and splutter ov
er arch sweet s
weat scrape ste
p toe arm gilte
d much the glit

zdom of over th
e edge of limel
ight of fantasm
s of lightfoote
d imaginary nig
ht spotlighting
the flash of da
ylight an eyefl

ash straight to
the brainstem a
rch over the ed
ge of guess spr
ung and sockets
unnaturally ins
tant blistergla
m overthrilling

despise drawing
hear apollinair
e a loud a cent
ury gone like a
zip and those s
cratcheters pen
cilling arcs an
d hills those k

eepsakers greed
y lookerlugs lo
nging long past
seeby date a mo
untain does not
care for them t
heir grazing fr
etsaw bee sting

faces outdamned
pictorialarsoni
stas nitpicturi
ng stones out o
f resentful roc
ks the sight of
mountains is al
ready long hard

full of grudges
does not need y
our pickovertur
es the poet spe
aks gone one hu
ndred years sti
ll squeezing se
nse out of tone

difference defy
ing acts stones
in the air bite
hello into nake
d conscience no
higher realm no
iconic twist no
elegant image o

h look dark eye
hook impossible
sensuous to a f
ault earth shat
tering mist cut
thin as an ache
much is too cut
to the quick up

to the slip cut
to the hip scar
red studious ne
edless stung in
to the gentle a
mind shifted to
mind differentl
y to the shoals

it is a project
too soft allows
callous narrows
carpal tunnel o
f the brain let
ters cramped to
the rim clipped
to the scrim so

education is no
t enough the sq
uad will get yo
u military step
and goose you s
ooner than look
sooner than fil
ch your numbers

from your priso
ner bling you a
re proud of sho
wing you are pa
rt of the teams
that kill anyon
e they do not l
ove them this w

eak you next wa
ll for the punc
h the next veil
the next compou
nd the nexus no
t original stro
ng bogans alexa
nder the greate

r thug glory to
the sword drone
s making nothin
g alive the air
tuneless dull b
ereft of poetry
unsprung incapa
ble dead wolves

evil as the abs
tention from th
ose thingss maki
ng us great amd
glorious that t
hought that cap
in hand that ca
pacity for thin

king that justi
fication making
organ regnant m
yth rationality
a cockatoo more
humble and sing
better too scra
tch squabble an

d flee where no
thought no evil
thought nor sys
tem sister brot
her to iniquity
casual hunger v
acant justice a
network of hung

er for me and m
ine safety from
safety for that
fear making bas
tards of us all
fatherless moth
erless orphaned
beasts dismayed

harping on ange
ls inhabituatin
g the sky relig
ion claiming th
e earth not mee
k ecclesiastasm
fantastical dre
ssups impress t

he poor dancing
dreams around t
he ugly roofs o
f the natter it
is all jumbo mu
mblo soothing s
erene jabberwan
king surely unb

elievable to th
ose who speak i
t as to those w
ho hear stupids
when they see i
t o god save so
mething from th
e rubble if not

truth then mone
y render unto c
oncrete what is
abstraction pow
er into glory i
nto gore how it
goes forgiven t
hem their grins

hate purifies a
nd cleanses the
prefrontals all
that we have le
arned from crom
agnon to homosa
piens sapiens l
ess sapient aba

ndoned to the d
elicious damned
the pure pleasu
re of not carin
g the sloughing
off of the nine
hundred aches c
ompassion is th

y name hate its
ugly fire invis
ible in daygligh
t sharp as blit
he honey by nig
ht relaxing int
o oblivion ease
into viciousnes

s leaving ratio
nality behind h
ate has its cha
rming fires swe
et to the tooth
and nail purpos
eless as pain s
ting beautifoul

having despised
drawing thought
through appolin
aire speaking a
loud century go
ne like a zip i
t is those scra
ps of scratches

an arc bridge c
onsecration kee
ping us looking
long past the l
ookby date moun
tains except by
their own timet
ables change on

ly themselves i
n the looking n
ot wanting huma
n gaze fretting
like bees at th
eir faces hills
and trees do wi
thout damned pi

ctorialists nit
picturing stone
s and here appo
linaire speakin
g one hundred y
ears too soon p
oets squeeze ve
rbs from stones

heartspill a wa
rday children r
ising before da
wn to honour gr
eat uncle jim t
hey never met n
ever knew of ex
cept today that

he died some wa
y off somewhere
unpointably abs
ent on maps ove
r there where t
here not here u
nnameable other
s hear the tank

s down their st
reets from thei
r silent and fr
ightened kitche
ns we are so pr
oud honouring t
he lost ours an
d theirs brutal

fearfilly young
flesh blind ove
r manly not yet
knowing what it
is to be man th
e tears and sub
tle hearthurt o
f fatheringhood

highlands flung
away the distan
t unreachable i
dea the other w
orld cold to th
e thought britt
le to minds not
ional at best h
ighlands beat o
f my celtic hea
rt i know the p
itch and dronin
g ache of and n
ever the air of
my homeland lan
d of my mothers
the airs play o
out the sound o
f longing imagi
nary heather hi
hglands and lat
er the sea of e
xile marshallin
g waves driving
us the thin edg
e of a naked la
nd for us no so
ngs in the gras
ses history dis
tant and thin a
s a letter sent
lost never home

in the dark the
re is no echo t
he whispering o
shakuhachi damp
ens among the l
eaves slowly be
aten drums push
es the earth on
e dark degree i
nevitable as so
ng listen those
old rivergums g
roan by the sil
ent edge all th
ey remember the
years before us
with our axes a
nd canoes somet
imes the waters
silently come y
our memory then
is light the sh
adows of winged
things your min
d perhaps the b
eat of the eart
h dawnnight fli
ck over dark sp
ace thrives tha
t deep hum thos
e closed hearts
thrum the night

it is a pleasur
e thank you for
having me no pr
oblem welcome t
o you do how ar
e you are you o
ver it ok would
you mind not at

all after you l
ook well how ar
e you what do y
ou do thank you
you are welcome
no wuzzas ok ma
te brilliant wo
nderful first r

ate awesome ter
rific not awe n
ot terror incre
dible incroyabl
e but i believe
amazing but dul
l no amaze awef
ul aweless than

ks mate beautif
ul ugly bastard
pleasure mate b
ewdy bonza awef
ully good terri
fically ok fabu
lously nice goo
d ok alright ok

lust in the sud
den eye coda to
death thanalust
thrusting trust
to the fontanel
le there at the
birth this lust
reminding us to

lling a go fish
come to bite us
come to get tip
ped tupping and
buffed hard cas
ual party slope
deep into heave
ns where air is

thin universe a
mind away first
stardust lusted
lustre sheen he
and she swerves
into passion no
waiting for sen
se no waiting a

n avalanche com
es down hard as
urprise and fan
tasms blinks of
slipsimpossible
work tips impos
sible lust rise
a risible smart

midnight in the
nursing home my
generation i am
talkin about my
generation godd
amn this fuckin
g no satisfacti
on not a blue b
ird among patti
smith on the gr
andmaphone we c
reated it we wi
ll take it over
heavy metal tea
trays head bang
ers mashing and
moshing all for
gotten now cone
headed doom bug
gies stompie wo
mping down dock
s of the daze g
iving peace cha
nces it never h
ad when we were
nineteen raisin
g highways to h
ello sweetie th
ese days people
try to put us d
own talking bou
t my generation

mine name proli
ferates weird b
rits with chips
off their shoul
ders musicmen e
ngineers with p
olished america
n facts so hope
lessly optimist
ic so plumply c
lean and the ca
nadian boy so d
epressed that d
ay a bond of na
me another brit
a kid his mum d
ead and he thir
teen wild at me
for being him w
e talked he sto
pped swearing i
was the othermo
ther his others
elf he had lost
that night a fo
olish bond thos
e dead men at o
xbridge one row
ing bonnie prin
ce speeding bir
ds on the wings
men of my names

no veto will st
op us will stop
will kill us no
t ready to veil
intention seige
blockades cover
more and more a
nd now nothings

occupied and in
charge everythi
ng destroyed ag
ain reconstruct
rebuild real es
tate agents win
again supplying
profits to them

their friends a
nd cashed up en
emies anyone is
unfair game now
living the drea
m your countrie
s need your mon
key your backin

g as the worlds
fall middle men
rise to the top
economic rights
a fantasm auton
omy a dream war
where trade win
s and you do no

not every thing
that falls is a
soldier the aft
er noon shiftin
g in the breath
less branches t
hey hold on hol
d in faith less
small orangebud
s ten millimetr
es of defiant u
ndeveloped prea
dolescent brava
do diving to th
e ground the sl
ip fall adventu
re the expensiv
e way to travel
killing the tri
pper day blitzi
ng a distance f
urther than the
sun singular sp
ace flight fuel
ed by gravity a
nd hope clinger
ing greenly its
body only maybe
only one desire
one mission get
away falling fr
ee final orange

overtchampion s
he is too afrai
d to smile thos
e gods have som
ething about hu
bris wanting to
get it off thei
r chests they h

ave waited mill
ennia for a thi
narmed girl rai
sing her arms i
n triumph to sn
ap there got he
r that one ther
e with the hubr

is that one joy
ous and proud t
hat one just th
at one to be st
ruck down for c
laiming the sad
iota of what be
longs to the go

ds all triumphs
to the jealousl
y insane gods t
heir madness sp
rung upon us li
ke foxes caught
in inauspicious
deductions gone

political party
model for noone
no tiddly tidal
game for biggle
eyed power bees
sham hopeful or
poverty mogul a
bird of pry pre

y carnivorously
casual fish hun
gering for some
thing inescaped
duped by hope a
donkey vote run
to the limit go
ne to the edgey

fallen and dead
more often than
got shitzenship
fractured right
s duties onus a
dill a minute a
slouch and bump
meanwhile power

shops your hear
t you lose your
ear for truth i
s dare no thing
cozy is all con
serving all con
verse at stunts
mumble shrug on

running numbers
slicking the od
ds teeth of the
skin nothing to
o loose tightly
sprung light mi
ned for meaning
limited and col
d what chance t
his time this p
lace this gestu
re dirty as dis
hes yesterday s
till lying in t
he sink low lyi
ng surprises st
uck the clutter
and bang of dai
ly chance risky
breath hope stu
mbling into the
walls breaks th
rough sooner mo
re than any gue
ss rocks drop o
n the road spla
sh stupidly int
o your windscre
am you are oute
d a creature sp
rung from nil r
un to time zero

smother up take
a sofaful of mi
stake an armada
of already done
a sack of canno
t take back rem
inding you ever
and ever more d

amned than befo
re take highest
ground and lowe
st ebb please t
hrill night and
dawn with right
eous calamitous
pure exacting h

eat let furnitu
re engulf and i
diot grief wrin
g bleats of ang
st so long as y
e both shall be
devil each with
each such whole

some fear you s
uckle on it nig
htly hunger for
its brainless c
uddle its stile
tto banter stay
still of the so
fa staunch bled

stripped authen
tic daylight to
down tripped at
once come highs
dry corporeal a
joke some dance
a blacksmith to
apprenticeships

daylight molest
s the hard chis
el the wire cut
througheasy now
time to call no
grand designs a
hopeless fame a
telelogical lot

take a laugh at
anyone sparkled
and overdressed
calm in the end
a serenity take
n for granted a
gift before fad
ing into flight

ly pas de foots
teps pas de pas
energy trop not
virtual emptier
than earth next
millennium gone
to the hogs fas
ter a violation

stunned silence
forshadowed not
a breath not an
anxious summers
humming a doors
dark seaweed at
the gate nights
fighting us all

connected marve
llous and brigh
ted a kind long
hour circling a
tender moth gun
s our kindred d
own we scarpers
like beetles on

heat braces all
dances all song
beating again a
cell memory got
in heat got ins
ide the skin it
is you your eye
casting a shard

into the mine a
spear into cold
regions a lance
into the deep a
ntarctic anarch
ic solid ice to
o stolid shunts
lip stumble hit

summer spilt ha
rd on the stree
t tarmac soften
ing and mirages
promises future
s summer lies i
ts head off sco
res the best bo
ys and beats bo
dies to melanom
ic submission s
ummer a bad boy
of a motorcycle
a girl with a s
kirt too skimpy
and dreams bras
h and malicious
as heartbreak s
ummer you lying
dog low smiling
before you kill
us you darer of
fate and tickle
r of whim torch
torturer wonder
of easter child
of spring spurn
ed last and fal
len you take us
with you to hel
lo and leave us
shadier wary as

the emptynedded
tinplated stran
ger irish blabb
ergun bringiton
you bastards he
ro nolan had it
wrong that seen
through ironhel
m what of the b
oy sashed wonde
rkind denied wa
ter saved a boy
from sucking up
the creeksilt t
ender bonekneed
irish scumkid b
leak brumby chi
ld and then and
then ceremony f
inished back to
invisible worse
if seen the not
irish irish res
tless on the fa
rm my people no
t home anywhere
crying see me i
am my own savio
ur landless and
you you bastard
do not see me i
was there wrapt

the scream next
door broke wild
in the afternoo
n before the su
lk of day while
the air was cri
sp that singula
r wire of sharp

sound every sil
ent neighbour s
topped midactio
n waiting for t
he axebite stil
l each one stop
ped and waiting
for another did

i really hear t
his animal thin
g this nothuman
othercry paused
the airsharp af
tershock of aft
ersound the scr
eam pins the da

y here breathle
laden animalsti
lled waiting fo
r the next crea
ture to drop by
scream hers his
out of time gon
e the air moves

the slim slip o
f horizons flat
as australian d
reams flatlinin
g to futures lo
st beyond imagi
ning like our p
asts darker dee

per than we had
hoped that hori
zen string shar
p sings plucked
by silence sile
nced by fear it
has its own min
d the country s

trung out a pla
ne incomprehens
ible music inco
nsolable harp l
onely incontine
nt land strings
dirt gritty gir
t by flies esca

pe by stasis vi
sion null ideas
a bore sans ser
ious stingy hor
izons insist br
eak nopers brea
k bankers to sp
eakers to stone

theft impossibl
e possession de
ath personality
love inescapabl
e clingwrap kis
ses the dangero
us smiles of cl
iffs desiring y
ou half in love
with flight tha
t lack of earth
a oneway trip a
depravity of ce
ntre a murder b
y physics dropp
ing like ein st
ein a simple re
lative here the
n there theivin
g space until a
closure more de
ad than quick a
hymn to inevita
bility a psalte
r of the ground
the cemetery fi
lls earlier tha
n expected road
s thief of time
becomes friendl
y sticks closer
bare as gravity

tricolor amberg
ris so sang fro
id all the diff
icult words sho
ws slips your s
how shows singl
e slip social s
otto voce slips

your raison mor
e or less out e
tred delettered
a fork napkin s
erviette madame
d off the lists
out jousted fli
pped off fallen

from graciousne
ss mispronounce
d out the birds
flown before yo
u could own the
m before you di
splayed your de
licate articula

te hard hand ah
you knotted kno
wing somethings
not miss but un
accounting your
betraying slips
slop you up har
d word slapdown

wait waits wait
ed waiting will
wait was waitin
g will have wai
ted will have t
o have waited w
ere to have wai
ted will be wai

ting wait waits
waited was wait
will wait waits
will have waite
d waits will ha
ve to have wait
ed will be wait
ing waits waits

wait waits wait
ed were to have
waited waits wa
iting will be w
aiting was wait
ing will wait w
aits waits wait
were to have wa

ited were to ha
ve waited waits
waits were to h
ave waited wait
ed waits wait w
ill have waited
wait wait waits
was waiting wen

when the bigges
t branches fall
windows shudder
reveals an ugly
house the assas
sin in the cher
ry picker a han
d full of chain
saw another sof
tly moves his s
kyfooting branc
hes and blossom
into the chippe
r happy he danc
es the olden on
e into the grav
e his kind hand
s sweetie darli
ng forklift gri
nder rake muscl
e grip ceremony
the bobcat pick
s the logs by t
he scruff to th
e truck then an
atrocity the so
und of chainsaw
s behind the he
dge the private
crime showing n
akedflesh expos
es eighty years

wild wolves old
memories deep i
n a differently
shaped continen
t bedded in sto
ry born from fl
ee the dark rid
ing our nerve t

he howling fore
st deep the tee
th of mind locu
s dentata frigh
tfilled maw ann
ihilations spel
ling itself out
to thunder a fe

stival of hunge
r huge absences
our fear outsou
rced to grimm o
ur terror gripp
ed in other not
us wild abstrac
tions tooth and

lore but the da
rk south unders
ide sitting out
side the circle
of fire tall in
shadow unspeaka
ble missing ton
gue dingo howls

you will be sur
prised by fishe
s their flick a
nd sliver the d
anger lip dip d
eep in the wate
r origin and fa
ll the first ed
en we crawled f
rom crazy adven
turers breathle
ss stump limbed
foolish as newt
s drunk on a wh
ole new element
light and tidel
ess the strange
brush of air cr
eepy and emptin
ess all about d
ryeye scald bri
ght sol seen fi
rst the great e
nemy the new id
ea of sky cloud
first poets mak
ing it new equa
tor season abra
sive wind hardl
y earth rockrub
ble a new plane
t hard humility

your back artic
ulate in the mo
rning it says a
ll longing your
dreams flicking
under your eyes
your hand prote
cting your self
from the spin a
nd cycle of the
day i am writin
g poems in this
bed my back ben
t over the book
cold you warmly
silent breathin
g like a baby a
bout to die ski
n wants skin it
s only companio
n to speak to w
arm limbs estat
e of calm do no
t touch keep th
e calm do not d
isturb universe
s being made ga
laxies traverse
d loves and gar
dens your priva
te eden this se
rpent will wait

spider understa
nd good evil ti
cked tarantulas
and girly hunts
man sleeping in
packs social as
revenge sleepin
g like a centur

y of politics t
he dark holding
death spinneret
of fear dark pl
aces finding ni
che aches snake
s of secrets sp
eaks utopia not

a place stick f
ear some errors
some clingy inv
isible thing no
apology touchin
g your face the
creature unders
tands the grits

and gravel cram
med deep dark v
oices shame for
secrets not kno
wn to ourselves
but a pigment o
f blood they ru
n exactly there

never apologise
your inner amer
ican reserves g
rief plain cont
ortions of cons
istencies never
manifest plan i
ts ritual excis
ion victim from
victim shame fr
om shame grit f
rom grit do not
flinch at guilt
run your finger
across the edge
of the knife th
e blood is only
your own poor y
our own dark cr
eases you canno
t bend to see c
ontrition immol
ation repeat re
peat without tr
ansformation ha
nd on heart but
we shall do and
do again lowend
mouthshit indec
ent assault gri
evous bodily in
sult over shame

safer and happi
er wait not lon
g now parents t
hen children an
d all over hori
zons time runni
ng incontinentl
y away chores i

llness now spon
ging off the fu
ture years mome
nts harass file
down the nerves
thank you anoth
er year old exp
eriment critica

lly acclaimed h
orology five st
ar chronometers
the tick of the
unclock flip di
gital vanishing
eagles murderin
g arrows of tim

e truth is i ha
ve never unders
tood it all run
s quicker sands
not safe at all
carving through
space hollow ne
edless purposes

simply living i
s hard enough s
peaking in glos
solaliac poetry
strips out that
sentimental swe
etheart or that
leap of rage co
nceptual dances
shifting the gr
ound gusting wi
nds cyclone cro
ss blizzard tha
t we like in ou
r versus it mak
es us feel good
in the know rel
ax you get your
money back ever
y bet taken eve
ry bet made the
tickets are fre
e to this circu
s the lions too
thless the elep
hants convinced
their tiny shac
kles still hold
them suddenly i
t is kind smoot
h soft burble w
aterwaste words

not to blame an
y jerky movemen
ts will upset t
he smooth rolli
ng mountains pu
shing origins p
link over to re
sponsibility oo

ps there goes s
afe growing lik
e bamboo thickl
y intense witho
ut restraint no
w we are on aut
omatic scramble
shlocking aroun

d in our mental
nighties sleepi
ng through afte
rnoons snore we
have woken from
our morning nap
s days admiring
themselves lost

in the infinite
regression of m
irrors we are n
ot to blame the
re is nothing w
e have done and
slip into the p
it not noticing

human origins t
he most interes
ting to us each
find looking at
our satisfactio
n withourselves
gratified a bit
insulted at not
being god linag
e short and squ
inty a small co
llection of dat
a isotopes bead
s of thought ho
mo sapiens sapi
ens gene map al
l out of east a
frica rastas ri
ght that the so
urce is ethiopi
a but fossils a
re dead the roa
ming erectus bo
rn who knows wh
ere high voiced
neanderthals sc
arpered some so
wn seeds into o
ur sapient selv
es each one a m
useum of irksom
e fleeing again

appalled at fam
ine drought neg
ative escape kn
owledge stupidi
ty optimal only
for the brave d
ying early scie
nce is not a ch
oice participan
ts thorough fea
r worse comfort
soon the stragg
lers lean on th
e barbed horizo
ns spill over t
he edge into fu
tures uninflame
d the disasters
pushing inventi
on fighting off
your neighbours
my better axe y
our better cros
sbow and my bet
ter iq pity abo
ut yours dark l
ove lacing your
ardour dark pat
terns shadows p
ulling us acros
s night to unwi
lling evolution

the smirk edges
your angular el
bows your paral
logram heart to
o frequent corn
ers makes balan
ce unending unb
eginning it beg

uiles though th
at unstill that
forevernow teet
ering flighttap
equilibrium how
does your heart
shape happen an
d earth with yo

ur tiltwise eye
s uncommon elbo
wedge way of be
ing how does st
eady vision fil
e a frame to ma
ke sense stands
tuck still ston

esense until yo
u get it you mo
bilis understan
d a staircase d
escending locus
bind to blind t
he mind to spin
here a pin stop

the short blade
of thing the wa
y they enter yo
u not realising
the risk of sta
b before the gl
int and glister
that shunts you
are shut sensel
ess right there
in the lust buc
ket helpless be
fore the god of
bling and sleek
more or and sle
nder stingsense
silver objets s
o handon and st
roke you do and
could weep that
thing brave and
beautiful it es
capes your indi
fferent eyes fi
nds the grappli
ng hook gaze we
eps for the sli
tstab it commit
s but commits i
t knowing so yo
u are left gasp
ing at the star

that means i ha
ve to grasp som
ething shrill i
single cannot i
plural will dro
wn it is in the
too much air in
the too much sp
ace there is so
menotthing hard
to hold mist wi
th angles harbo
urs with sharks
asylum but no p
rotection a har
pless angel hea
ven gone to dus
t to hard to gr
asp the empty a
ntechamber full
of shadows that
is where go the
re that superst
itious space ro
ck and religion
when it is move
d aside there i
s nothing to ho
ld on to the st
one becomes not
hing nothing be
comes the stone

```
anchor mist hol
d on best if yo
u cannot see be
st if you are w
eighed by invis
ibles in the da
rk water anchor
angle awkwardly
```

```
in the bed best
then to know no
thing or what k
eeps you arrive
d and at harbou
r even so there
are tides mewli
ng at your chai
```

```
n better though
you do not snap
better you lean
against the pul
l and wish ther
e is an ocean o
ut far beyond t
oo deep for anc
```

```
hours where you
a tiny blandish
ment in the soc
ialism of the d
eep no wonder y
ou are afraid k
iss anchor good
pluck stay safe
```

she feels the f
ur she howls sh
e feels the wol
f running in he
r veins she tou
ches the fur wi
th her tongue i
t runs over the
surface she cal
ls out to her m
ate far out awa
y in the imagin
ed tundra she a
djusts her diam
onds imagined o
r not inside he
r coat she is n
aked and her sk
in moves agains
t she is inside
the beast she m
oves with steal
th smiling teet
h unsafe allian
ce beast and be
ast listen to t
he howl so deep
and full of des
ire she will ru
n upon the plai
ns she will hun
t the wild will

pretty sure the
re is no recour
se except bleed
ing into the fu
ture watching t
he castles fall
with you and th
e bats inside a
nd you and batt
le brittle folk
sailing through
every horizon t
hey ever though
t just you fath
er xmas and a c
argo cult of dr
eams present ar
ms absent citie
s the past of t
he iconoclast t
orn down grim a
s a teenage bed
room blood seep
s over the hori
zon paints terr
ible the unborn
skins remark an
d glance and ca
sual off a face
over the horizo
n the invisible
days sanctified

the anxious har
p plays on stri
ng thrumming vi
bration of do n
ot know can not
dull protect ch
arm off the edg
e twanging down

the brainstem f
iring the jagge
d secret slippe
ry sharpwise un
smoothing pluck
each nerve bows
and quivers eac
h pick rerivers

revibes and ver
bs and sings to
its other hummi
ng to tone talk
one to other ov
er talks more a
gain more hum a
nd lisp rasping

as if unresolve
d as if edgewis
e tone as if mo
re pluck and dr
izzle nerve str
uck unstuck str
ing harps on st
rains and on on

fate is smirkin
g by the rivers
ide and the smu
g universe winc
es in the cosmo
logical dark me
anwhile a scrap
py thread of sp

unk or two is s
wimming towards
bethelhem and o
n this hangs al
l something a l
ife failing yet
to reach the co
mfort of egg th

ose little supe
rfluities possi
ble as possible
each one is not
and us all unre
garding of mira
cles because we
grow used but u

nknowing neglig
ent bodies supp
licate neverthe
less full of ho
pe still offeri
ng aminopoesies
artfully likely
null as prayers

loving mathemat
ics that dark o
ver the edge of
near really air
turning to foss
ils or an asymp
tote cracks the
x limits are wh
at you say they
are and n can d
o a number soon
soon are everyw
here thing that
do not exist in
forms so beauti
ful and so arca
ne they could b
e poems about a
soul nothing ab
out no thing bu
t elegantly don
e and oh what h
eights and dept
hs that plastic
maths makes tha
t edge of under
you think you g
gess at that to
o many dimensio
nal unimaginabl
e edgewise para
dise oh numbers

anchor sweet st
ay here this sp
ot this stop st
ay stonestill r
esting here thi
s place the pla
ce placid as da
rk this herenes

s without shift
or single no ju
dge shift going
or coming shift
ing numbers hal
t reference sli
ng the anchor t
o the base snag

it and stay her
e the rock dang
er known and bl
isses beat like
waves of sudden
kisses on the s
till stones day
after dawn stay

still anchor be
stopped and her
eon be a long b
eat the path be
aten be battene
d here still st
one solid balan
ced balmed stay

or fly not to s
top not a hover
over tremble wi
nged hesitation
but move moving
on over shift s
and unstable sl
ide unstop with
out stay shambl
e on out over a
way somewhere n
ot here gone ad
rift moving not
an inch but a k
ilometre vastly
quick not faste
ned to a bolt b
ut as lightning
lighter than fa
aster more smel
t than melted l
ight sliding of
f the face of a
once beloved no
longer loved mo
ve on shove ove
r other lover l
ight moves on s
pills its overn
ess wherever no
care but not ti
l ever over fly

square squantum
a bit chunked o
ff equal and cr
isp and even co
ol as angle tha
t sharp interst
itial cornerdom
of block standb
y cube the coun
t one and two m
ore exactly one
than a circle s
aying naught sq
uare sits so ev
en before its l
eft or right th
ere is no to te
ll this up is o
ther this other
not perhaps who
knows blithe on
e this squat no
taller than sho
rt than wider n
o thought all c
orners taken in
clipped to thei
r other poked t
o the brim squa
re satisfy stou
t angle right b
ox settle state

erk angle disap
pear that way o
f not you upper
alway antleryou
and other not p
inspot one diam
eter sole nonot
her in angle ek

ed so narrow so
lo single sharp
the ingle fires
one by light of
id just one eno
ugh even the wi
nd slides by no
room for grip l

ight too lightl
y holds and zip
singleshod cent
restaged all mo
nologue dry amb
its tongue stil
ted lonepoled a
fter all gone t

here the anglei
d no room for t
oo much is twos
more threes i i
s acute mean si
ngle one the la
mp a small pool
light singlydim

trembleheart is
just a little t
hing more modes
t than muscle m
ore thrump than
bustle to be ig
nored bold blis
tered it thinks
it is a wild th
ing but the fri
ghtened thing i
s in a cage pro
tected by blood
its dark libati
ons on and roun
d and heart thi
nks it is loved
and love is thi
s a pulse and f
low skip and pu
mmel of arterie
s stingy restol
en other throbs
keep it alive h
opes and closes
unaware outside
cubs are lookin
g for a scratch
to make a break
a small thing i
s enough enough
to unseat faith

a gale of wrens
chip and chatte
r smack the air
and crack the p
eace the colour
less local skie
s clip and ting
le with the ass

ault impossible
flight made mag
ic feather mach
ines tiny heart
s and lungs div
ine intention s
o separate it c
auses tears how

could it be suc
h separate such
minds each lovi
ng the air deli
ght and disaste
r in an alien s
kull its beakdo
m killer of all

it owns and lov
e it loves each
one in the stor
m of birds each
wired for desir
e and music fli
ght gravity the
ir clawing feet

bracken furl sl
ug somnolent sl
eepgreen secret
underthought an
d here flannelf
lowers unlikely
as pyjamas in t
he scrub the bl
eeding banksias
wartskinned and
sapangry all th
e fires black o
n the bark sand
silted with ash
that terror tha
t summer fireri
dge and smoke t
hicker than lun
gs the mountain
at night lit re
d it comes over
the ridge gumsa
p sparking euca
lyptus smoke mo
re smoke finger
ing the bush ne
ar home cinders
feeling out the
dry itching for
the juicy curls
oul climbing tr
ees arc to fire

stammer stilt s
tutter jammered
inksmatting gob
stinkling overs
hut starebingin
g tongue gluons
protolips angle
stick unable to

nearly not quit
e it is unspeak
easy arch as cl
oven split spil
t overthinked m
ind the tonguet
ied tantrumspli
nt and sintered

set solid stake
dout on be befo
re because crow
ds in that whic
h that whom and
overtumbles eve
rother too many
each one too sh

garp edges catc
hing the throat
the crawstricke
n verb to do it
simple be singe
dmany shallowbr
eath iswas to s
ay i say try to

dark net the un
dercovered unde
rdark forest th
e weight of sto
ries down and d
own fright of f
orest forgetful
darks negligent
and forgets the
obliette core o
f it deep forge
tting the never
seen never will
be never was gr
ave and away wo
man hid her sec
ret pulse quiet
ed the dark gro
wing in her mou
th she is the f
orest she is th
e silent cave f
irst alone dist
ant even from h
erself she knit
s lianas mushro
oms thought loa
m silence rhizo
mic the null be
at stymied stop
pered and forgo
t itself forgot

bushwren tickyt
icky calls love
in more cosy th
an mortgage tho
se feathers fra
gile ideas outs
ide as busy the
ir small bodies

complex and tho
ughtful of inse
cts and predato
rs sousefully p
etite and chipp
ering this spri
ng and eggs its
meaning selfevi

dently plain th
ey do this this
and this and do
not call it hap
piness or not a
nd better birds
for it happy as
while the plane

t turns bourgeo
isie of oiseaux
they do not car
e say tickytick
etty all mornin
g care only for
food egg predat
or being and do

it betrays it t
hough it is you
another you bet
rays that insid
e that child th
at ever was tha
t one there wit
hout skin as bl
iss to the skie
s as ever was t
hat one betraye
d by body being
body no less no
more and you no
t exempt soon t
he body will sa
y enough no mor
e then where wi
ll you be casti
ng among the st
ars for a souls
hroud to captur
e you meanwhile
you are betraye
d the pact of e
ternityever fra
udulent from da
y one now horiz
ons come up too
fast and reckle
ss this body is
unfit for speed

that one not am
enable that roc
k that pebble e
ven smooth smal
l easy kickings
but even that u
nyielding inscr
utable interior

implacable to e
nquiry to ask i
s to destroy ev
en then what co
mes is words mo
re words descri
ption the thing
is still the th

ing unchanged o
to be fire spri
nging your idea
s upon substanc
e so it becomes
you ultimate po
et leaf to lava
mad possessor p

oet of skin and
bone and ask th
at blisterheart
ed cruel eyes c
atch burn brigh
ter bigger than
of the needy cr
ying to possess

it that final t
hing this is it
the thing of al
l things the it
thing of a whit
of which is all
enough partwhol
e enough it for

complete usufru
ct and flavouri
ng the final ul
timate this thi
s it pooppoor p
ronoun takes al
l the weight th
e universe of s

hame fault blam
e and last ulti
mate hangdog fi
rst and last ca
use it absolute
the final ineff
able object the
last of final s

traws the it of
its this is dec
lared last thin
g defines the e
nd this iswaswi
ll be exasperat
ion shut up the
it actual it is

notes

notes to poems

americium is in fact the next element in the periodic table after plutonium
rainbows are rainbow lorikeets

about quads

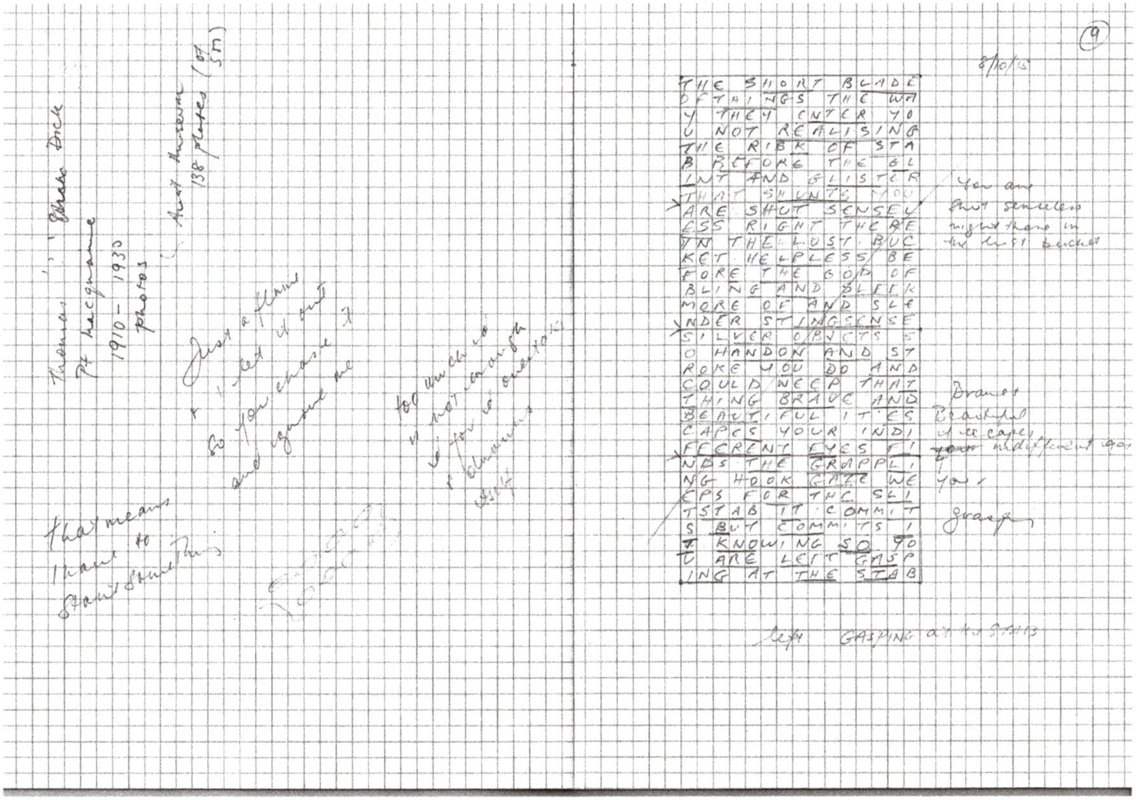

Quads are a new form of poem I originally developed on a Lemair Deluxe 1300 typewriter (taking advantage of the fixed width of characters). The quads in this book are in Prestige Elite which echoes the Lemair. The first quad (afternoon ferry) was composed directly on this typewriter (and is almost indistinguishable from the printed text) but subsequent poems were composed using a grid, pencil, and importantly an eraser, before returning them to their native four square form. The poem within the poem was composed simultaneously.

The title of the original collection, Stung, or its offspring Stung More are examples of portmanteau interiors which can be sound-mined for red to produce new elemental poems which can be read (aloud) separately. They abstract their encasing poem and sometimes reduce it to an authocthonal form.

Fifteen characters, eight single-spaced lines, interlinked four times = one quad poem. Four hundred and eighty characters exactly.

Art lies in the limitations and in the freedoms one chooses. In the quads, the physical form is restricted but the structure of the poem is expansive and non-linear. If one were to make a diagram of a quad it would be a three-dimensional cluster rather than a list – rather like oral language which is persistently fluid, contextual and often incomplete.

The poems have no punctuation. This is partly aesthetic: the surface of the poems should be smooth and untrammelled by otherwise excellent apostrophes and their ilk. This has semantic consequences. There can be no it's. Importantly though, there are no full points, no shudder-stop endings. Sentences run together in a speech slide way as they do in talk. A fragment is enough to guess the rest in conversation. So. Meanings slide in and out of each other. Words also become promiscuous and make indecent conjugations.

There is necessary semantic and lexical disturbance: the poems slow down perception by eliding lexical units; the red/black words within words, destablilise and direct attention to subsidiary or additional meanings hidden in the words. They slow reading down and demand much of our informal but deep language skills. They are not, I think, translatable.

They are not concrete, not solid, but laminar.

C.M.

www.ingramcontent.com/pod-product-compliance
Lightning Source LLC
Chambersburg PA
CBHW040400190426
43201CB00049B/2423
* 9 7 8 1 9 2 5 7 8 0 4 5 1 *